my theology

The Audacity
of Peace

MY theology

Scot McKnight

The Audacity of Peace

Blessings
Scot McKnight
Mk 12:29-31

Fortress Press
Minneapolis

THE AUDACITY OF PEACE

Originally published by Darton, Longman, and
Todd London, UK
Copyright © 2022 Scot McKnight. Published by
Fortress Press, an imprint of 1517 Media.
All rights reserved.
Except for brief quotations in critical articles or reviews,
no part of this book may be reproduced in any manner
without prior written permission from the publisher. Email
copyright@1517.media or write to Permissions, Fortress
Press, PO Box 1209, Minneapolis, MN 55440-1209.

Print ISBN: 978-1-5064-8457-0
eBook ISBN: 978-1-5064-8458-7

Cover design: Kristin Miller

Contents

Preface — 7

1. Sider — 13
2. Bonhoeffer — 31
3. Gorman and Bonhoeffer — 57
4. Craigie — 71
5. Collins — 85

Preface

THE TWENTIETH CENTURY was the bloodiest century to date. Some 155 million persons died in what American conservative *Washington Post* columnist George Will calls the 'scalding obscenity' of war.[1] I was there for half of that twentieth century. My Viet Nam draft number was number 151. The year they drafted those born in my birth year, 1953, the United States Selective Service reached 95. The last draft was in December of 1972 and the authority to induct American young men was over June 30, 1973. The Viet Nam Conflict came to an end, if 'end' is what we want to call it. War, even if called a 'Conflict', never comes to an end: the

[1] George F. Will, *American Happiness and Discontents* (New York: Hachette, 2021), 62.

dead don't come back to life and soldiers suffer PTSD, as Roger Benimoff's searing memoir, *Faith Under Fire*, shows. One of my childhood friends I played baseball with at times is now an engraved name on the wall in Washington, D.C..

I cannot pretend even to have been all that informed about the morality of war or the Viet Nam Conflict when I was a teenager. What I knew was that they could send me a letter of induction and I would be on my way. In fact, I was politically aloof. I was stunned by the Kent State massacre and the My Lai massacre. These were two events of the Viet Nam era that shaped my generation's posture toward militarism and war. My year for the draft came and went. I was never involved in an anti-Viet Nam protest. The American military learned very little from the Viet Nam Conflict, globally evident by our reckless invasion of both Iraq and Afghanistan. International saviors save little and sin lots.

By the end of the 1970s, and thus too late to have made a difference for the Viet Nam era, I had begun to think through the Christian's relationship to war and America's militarism.

THE AUDACITY OF PEACE

This book tells a story of wending my way to a fixed peace ethic about war, about gun ownership, about the death penalty, about abortion, and about inhumane treatment of prisoners – to use the language of many today, I seek to be consistently pro-life, to believe in the possibility of human transformation, reconciliation, restoration, and all manner of peace-making and peace-building. I won't even discuss most of these life issues, but I see them as instances of a larger theme: peace.

Peace is worth fighting for. It's a war I have waged – silently, verbally, and in writing – for nearly fifty years. Once when I was lecturing at a school, was asked a question about the Iraq invasion. When I said I was against it and was a pacifist someone at the back of the room raised his voice in opposition and yelled a few words at me. I did my best to work for some peace. He was a 'realist' and accused me of being a 'utopian'. I am not a utopian. I don't think empires will succumb to the peace witness. I am a Christian. I am a peace witness. I don't witness to peace to win the world but to offer a Christian alternative to the 155 million deaths in twentieth-century wars. This small book records some of my journey.

A summary statement

A peace ethic embodies the self-denial ethic of Jesus. A peace ethic volitionally and communally participates in the cruciform pattern of the life of Jesus. Through the power of God's grace and the indwelling Spirit of God the participant in the way of Jesus is transformed into a Christoform life.

The threshold moment for this at the ethical level is found in two statements in the Book of Acts:

> But Peter and John answered them, 'Whether it is right in God's sight to listen to you rather than to God, you must judge' (Acts 4:19).

> But Peter and the apostles answered, 'We must obey God rather than any human authority' (Acts 5:29).

THE AUDACITY OF PEACE

In the second century Tertullian responded to some Christian 'realists' who knew military service was financially profitable with a warning that echoes the words of these apostles:

> There can be no compatibility between the divine and the human sacrament [pointing to the military oath], the standard of Christ and the standard of the devil, the camp of light and the camp of darkness (see *De Idolatria* 19:1-20).[2]

A twentieth-century peace witness, Magda Trocmé, said the same in a new context with these words: 'There are no war crimes. War is the crime.'[3]

I have responded to Tertullian's call and I agree with Magda Trocmé. Warring and the

---

[2] Translation taken from George Kalantzis, *Caesar and the Lamb: Early Christian Attitudes on War and Military Service* (Eugene, Oregon: Cascade, 2012), 57.

[3] As heard by Peter Rose, recorded in the Foreword to R. P. Unsworth, *A Portrait of Pacifists: Le Chambon, the Holocaust, and the Lives of André and Magda Trocmé* (Syracuse, New York: Syracuse University Press, 2012), xi.

Christian faith are incompatible. As I said above, I wended my way to these choice and to that journey I now turn, focusing on the thinkers that shaped a peace ethic.

1
Sider

ONE CAN DRAW a straight line from Leo Tolstoy to Mahatma Gandhi, and then from Gandhi to Martin Luther King, Jr.. Walk that line and you will also meet Dietrich Bonhoeffer and Michael Gorman and forms of pacifism, radical and resistant and political and prophetic. Though I have learned from each of these, pacifism first entered my conscience through an American Mennonite, Ronald Sider.

In the late 1970s I read Sider's *Rich Christians in an Age of Hunger* and began to read into the ways of the Anabaptists. Kris and I, along with our small children, participated for a couple of years in a Catholic Worker home called 'Anawim House', where I began to develop a social conscience both about possessions and war. The leaders, Pat and Mary Murray, owned a small bookshop and Pat regularly informed me of new books that could help me in my journey. One of these was Ronald Sider's lectures called *Christ and Violence*, a short book that converted me to a peace ethic in a single reading.[4]

In what follows I reflect on Sider's study. There is no attempt here to reconstruct what I believed in those days, other than the transformative encounter I had reading *Christ and Violence*. My mind changed. Rather, I reflect on what I think now about a theme I first learned in Sider's book, sticking to some kind of reflection on what he wrote. In one brief formula:

Christ chose the cross, not the sword.

Jesus' approach to victory was not a war, not to be armed, not to fight but to die, to give himself for others. In Sider's words, 'Christians who reject violence follow the way of the cross rather than the way of the sword'.

[4] Ronald J. Sider, *Christ and Violence* (Scottdale, Penn.: Herald Press, 1979).

The World of Jesus

At the time of Jesus a sect was alive and well at Qumran that had a scroll we now call *The War Scroll*, and that sect had an apocalyptic hope, a fantasy really, of a final military battle in which the sons of light would annihilate the sons of darkness. Alongside that sect at the time of Jesus the zealot option was surging. The zealots believed in the story of Phinehas, the priest, who was commended for the use of violence to restore faithful observance of the Torah (Numbers 25:1-13; Psalm 106:28-31). They also knew the stories of the Maccabees, who resisted the Seleucid takeover and defilement of the temple by taking up arms and recapturing Jerusalem for the observance of the Torah (1-2 Maccabees). They also knew the Psalms of Solomon vision for the Messiah.

> Behold, O Lord, and raise up to them their king, the son of David, at the time, in the which you choose, O God, that he may reign over Israel your servant. And gird him with strength, that he may

shatter unrighteous rulers. And that he may purge Jerusalem from nations that trample (her) down to destruction. In the wisdom of righteousness he will thrust out sinners from (the) inheritance, He will destroy the pride of the sinner as a potter's vessel. With a rod of iron he will break in pieces all their substance. He will destroy the godless nations with the word of his mouth. At his rebuke nations will flee before him. And he will reprove sinners for the thoughts of their heart. And he will gather together a holy people, whom he will lead in righteousness. And he will judge the tribes of the people that has been sanctified by the Lord his God. And he will not suffer unrighteousness to lodge any more in their midst, nor will there dwell with them any man that knows wickedness. For he will know them, that they are all sons of their God. And he will divide them according to their tribes upon the land. And neither sojourner nor alien will sojourn with them any more. He will judge peoples and nations in the wisdom of his righteousness. Selah. (*PsSol* 17:21-29; Craig Evans et al.; Accordance Bible Software).

No matter how you shake that text, what spills out of the bag is a violent Messiah, and this too was a major expectation for the world in which Jesus was nurtured. Resistance occurred, but mostly it was futile. Rome had conquered the land in 63BC, had grown into an empire by the time of Jesus and had strategically placed in the area power brokers of Rome – think Herod the Great, Pilate, and Herod Antipas. Taxation was a constant irritation, famines exacerbated the irritations, and at times it all bubbled up into a foment of resistance. People like the sign prophets of Josephus or the zealots like Judas – and many more whose names are not recorded in documents – produced a world in which heroes could be made by simple acts of rebellion and resistance.

Jesus taught God's empire (or kingdom) in this context.

The Way of Jesus

Two disciples, James and John, wanted to sit at the left and right of Jesus in that kingdom. Testing them, he asks if they actually think they can endure what he will endure. They think they can. He knows otherwise. Actually, he knows they too will be martyred, but what he can't do is assign them such seats of power. Such places are designated by God. So Mark 10:35-40. The other ten apostles were indignant about the hubris of the brothers.

Jesus informs them that desiring seats of power is the way of Rome and its pawns (10:42). Second, he clears out a completely different path for the disciples:

> But it is not so among you; but whoever wishes to become great among you must be your servant, and whoever wishes to be first among you must be slave of all. For the Son of Man came not to be served but to serve, and to give his life a ransom for many. (All translations of the Bible are from the New Revised Standard Version.)

If they are going to follow him, as they had chosen from the very beginning (cf. John 1:35-51; Mark 1:16-20; Luke 5:1-11), they will follow one whose path is the Way of the Cross.

The Way of the Cross begins with one's posture: one must choose the discipline of serving others instead of power over others, instead of leading, one is to be a follower of Jesus. The desire is not to be 'great' or 'first' but instead to be 'servant' (*diakonos*) and 'slave' (*doulos*). Jesus himself did not come to 'be served but to serve' and his service required that he 'give his life as a ransom for many' (10:43-45). We can dispute whether 'ransom' means substitution or liberation, and whether 'for' means 'instead of' or 'for the benefit of', but the impact is that Jesus' death saves humans from their condition and then transforms them into a life of serving others. One can't dominate people and serve them at the same time.

What I learned from Sider is that *Jesus here consciously and intentionally rejected the way of violence and power over others and chose the way of suffering and service as the path to 'victory', now redefined.* One doesn't get to the Easter victory of Jesus apart from the defeat on Friday.

These words confirm what Jesus had taught and would teach in other settings. At the Temptation he rejects the 'glory' and 'authority' to rule 'all the kingdoms of the world' that Satan can grant him if he will be bow to the devil (Luke 4:5-8). His first sermon in Nazareth, expounding as it did Isaiah 61, articulates a mission of 'good news to the poor' and to 'captives' and to the 'blind' and to the 'oppressed' (4:18). When Jesus provoked the disciples to name who he was in Israel's story, Peter declares him to be 'Messiah of God' (9:20). But Jesus immediately 'sternly ordered' them into silence and revealed to them the Way of Jesus: 'The Son of Man must undergo great suffering, and be rejected by the elders, chief priests, and scribes, and be killed, and on the third day be raised' (9:22). Messiah he is, but not the Messiah of their fathers' world. He would be a crucified Messiah who would revolutionize the very meaning of Messiah.

Jesus called people to follow him. And the 'him' who was to be followed was the crucified one.

> If any want to become my followers, let them deny themselves and take up their cross daily and follow me (Luke 9:23).

The Way of Jesus is the Way of the Cross. The path of honor walks with Jesus toward Golgotha and it means being ashamed of the way of Rome's mighty powers. Beyond the cross, beyond the shame, and beyond serving others is the kingdom of God.

Jesus embodied the Way of the Cross in a way that subverted the way of Rome and the rulers when he entered Jerusalem to the fanfare of a few disciples. His approach was from the east and he rode not a mounted steed in armor, but a donkey (Luke 19:28-40). Not long after he is back on the other side of the eastern slope in Gethsemane. Judas leads a crowd and emerges to kiss Jesus to identify Jesus to those who would arrest Jesus. The question is asked of him, 'Lord, should we strike with the sword?' (22:49). When the moment was ripe to use the force of a sword, Jesus denied that power, knowing his path would lead into the heart of the Roman and Judean power and it would lead to prosecution, trial, and crucifixion.

But Sunday morning's sunrise followed Friday evening's darkness. Victory comes through the Cross and reveals the Way of the Cross as the Way of Jesus for all his followers, including the apostles. As Sider said, the redemptive nature of the death of Jesus never stopped the Christians from perceiving the cross also as an ethic.[5]

The Way for Followers

An early Christian hymn, Philippians 2:6-11, expresses the habit of the cross. When the Philippians were at one another's throats Paul calls attention to their 'hymnbook', page one, the song about 'Christ Jesus'.

[5] Sider, 35.

THE AUDACITY OF PEACE

Who, *though* he was in the form of God,
did not regard equality with God
as something to be exploited,
but emptied himself,
taking the form of a slave,
being born in human likeness.
And being found in human form,
he humbled himself
and became obedient to the point of
 death —
even death on a cross.
Therefore God also highly exalted him
and gave him the name
that is above every name,
so that at the name of Jesus
every knee should bend,

in heaven and on earth and under the earth,
and every tongue should confess
that Jesus Christ is Lord,
to the glory of God the Father.

I have since learned from Michael Gorman's fine studies on cruciformity that 'though' (in italics) may be translated otherwise.[6] Woodenly we could translate 'being in the form of God.' Gorman prefers 'because', in which case the cross reveals not a concession by God ('though') but the very heart of God (because the cross is what God is like). Our God is a cruciform God and the cross is not just an instrument of redemption but a revelation of the Revealer! The way to the throne room with God is not the sword but the cross. To follow Jesus is to follow precisely *that* Jesus.

From Philippi to Rome, a wannabe colony to the real thing. What Paul knows about the assemblies of Jesus in Rome includes some deep divisions between those he calls the Weak and Strong, which is better translated the 'Powerful' and the 'Powerless', the Powerful being the gentile believers now in charge of the Jewish believers in Jesus.[7] Each

[6] Michael J. Gorman, *Inhabiting the Cruciform God: Kenosis, Justification, and Theosis in Paul's Narrative Soteriology* (Grand Rapids: Wm. B. Eerdmans, 2009).

[7] Scot McKnight, *Reading Romans Backwards: A Gospel of Peace in the Midst of Empire* (Waco, TX: Baylor University Press, 2019).

claims some power to shape the other, one side wanting freedom with respect to foods and Sabbath practices while the other wants more Torah observance by gentile believers. What's Paul's solution? Like Jesus, 'Put down the swords! Surrender one to another' (Romans 14:1-15:13). The essential practice for Paul was the subversion of power claims by welcoming one another to the table and eating with one another as siblings instead of as rivals to righteousness (14:1; 15:1-2). Why? Because laying down ourselves for the other is the Way of Christ: 'For Christ did not please himself; but, as it is written, "The insults of those who insult you have fallen on me".' (15:3). Paul appeals to the Way of the Cross as the new messianic paradigm.

Peter, too. A 'biblical biography' of Peter includes his repudiation of the words of Jesus about dying at the hands of the rulers (Mark 8:32-33; omitted in Luke 9) as well as his denials of Jesus during his trials (Luke 22:54-62). Something transforming happens to Peter at Pentecost (Acts 2) and by the time he writes his letters the man has embraced the cross as the paradigm of the Christian life. Slaves are to endure what they cannot resist by turning toward the Way of the Cross with Jesus (1 Peter 2:18-25).

It must be emphasized that this teaching of Jesus, which I have increasingly learned as needed any time this is taught, does not legitimate abuse or mistreatment. Nor does it oppose opposing what can be opposed. More of this kind of nonviolent resistance later, but I want to caution readers about the potential misuse and abuse of these words. The Way of the Cross is not a legitimation of interpersonal violence but the *choice by free willing individuals to absorb the heat as a witness to the Way of Jesus.*

Sider, at the end of his first major chapter, summarized it in a way that summarizes what I have said so far: 'Jesus' cross, where He practiced what He had preached about love for one's enemies, becomes the Christian norm for every area of life.'[8] In my own journey into pacifism a turn on the road occurred when I

[8] Sider, *Christ and Violence*, 38.

read Sider's *Christ and Violence* and saw, as if for the first time, the Way of the Cross as the Way of Jesus. When the Cross becomes the paradigm for how to relate to others, including both siblings in Christ and international public relationships, I was on a path to a principled pacifism.

Behind Sider stood another Mennonite. That man, tragically, was a serial sexual abuser of women as well as an author of a book that shaped the minds of many, including mine. His hypocrisy and mendacity grieve me to the point that I no longer will cite him. Behind him was a French activist of protecting Jews escaping Hitler, a man named André Trocmé.[9] These thinkers shaped many of us by calling our attention to the Sermon on the Mount as the ethical vision of Jesus for kingdom people.

---

[9] André Trocmé, *Jesus and the Nonviolent Revolution*, trans. Michael H. Shank and Marlin E. Miller (Scottdale, Penn.: Herald Press, 1973).

2
Bonhoeffer

AS A COLLEGE STUDENT I routinely visited a large Christian bookstore in downtown Grand Rapids. The bookstore manager once mentioned to me that I would benefit from reading Dietrich Bonhoeffer's *The Cost of Discipleship*. As a sophomore or junior in college I read that book for the first time. Much of it flew at a level I could not then reach but that book transformed me because in the heart of that book is a short exposition of the Sermon on the Mount. (My green paperback from Macmillan eventually fell apart from my usage of it, I bought another one and it too shows plenty of signs of wear. But that book's best version is now called *Discipleship* in the complete works of Bonhoeffer, which I cite from in this book.)

At the time I did not know the depth of Bonhoeffer's thinking but I now understand him better, at least I think I do:[10]

> [On the 'eye for an eye' saying] Jesus releases his community from the political and legal order, from the national form of the people of Israel, and makes it into what it truly is, namely, the community of the faithful that is not bound by political or national ties (132).

I was aware enough of German history to catch the significance of 'political and national' but the potency of this Lutheran theologian's countering of nothing less than national consciousness should stun the reader.

> Evil will become powerless when it finds no opposing object, no resistance, but, instead, is willingly borne and suffered (133).

Only one who has absorbed Bonhoeffer's sense

---

[10] All page numbers in parentheses are from Dietrich Bonhoeffer, *Discipleship*, Dietrich Bonhoeffer Works 4 (Minneapolis: Fortress, 2001).

of responsibility to Germany and to the church, as well as his deep thinking on 'guilt', can tap into the significance of this line. But the statement enters into Bonhoeffer's theory of discipleship as entering to the life of Christ and love of enemy.

> With his command Jesus calls disciples against into communion with his passion (136).

> Loving one's enemies leads disciples to the way of the cross and into communion with the crucified one (141).

These few quotations, taken from Bonhoeffer's commentary on the last parts of Matthew 5, led me into pondering Bonhoeffer's own understanding of how to follow Christ in Nazi Germany. More importantly, he gave me a life-long love for the fierceness of the Sermon on the Mount.[11] Which Sermon helped shape me into a peace ethic.

---

[11] Scot McKnight, *The Sermon on the Mount*, Story of God Bible Commentary (Grand Rapids: Zondervan, 2013).

What didn't fly over my head ...

Bonhoeffer had a revealing conversation about the assassination of Hitler. The conversation was reported by Wolf-Dieter Zimmermann.[12] As an illegal pastor in Werder on the Havel, Zimmermann reports that in 1942 Bonhoeffer and some friends joined Zimmermann for an evening at his home. A dramatic moment occurs when Werner von Haeften asks a silencing question. As a staff lieutenant in the Third Reich's Army High Command, von Haeften turns to Bonhoeffer and asks:

> Shall I shoot? I can get inside the Führer's headquarters with my revolver. I know where and when the conferences take place. I can get access.

Zimmermann tells us the conversation over that question 'lasted for many hours'. But

---

[12] Wolf-Dieter Zimmermann and Ronald Gregor Smith, eds., *I Knew Dietrich Bonhoeffer*, trans. Käthe Gregor Smith (New York: Harper & Row, 1966), 190–192.

Zimmermann also summarized Bonhoeffer's answer:

> Bonhoeffer explained that the shooting by itself meant nothing: something had to be gained by it, a change of circumstances, of the government. The liquidation of Hitler would in itself be no use; things might even become worse. That, he said, made the work of the resistance so difficult, that the 'thereafter' had to be so carefully prepared.

Zimmermann continues by turning back to von Haeften's measured comments. He was 'from an old officers' family, was a gentle type, enthusiastic, idealistic, but also a man of Christian convictions who believed in inherited traditions. He was one of Niemöller's confirmands.' Zimmermann reports that at this point von Haeften 'suddenly developed enormous energy' and pushed harder, wanting to know what was right to do. 'Bonhoeffer, on the other hand, exhorted him over and over again to be discreet, to plan clearly and then to see all unforeseen complications through. Nothing should be left to chance.' One senses the emotional moment when von Haeften again pushes for an answer: 'Shall I...? May I ...?'

At this moment Bonhoeffer's response is reveals both his approach to pacifism and the very personal nature of discernment. 'Bonhoeffer,' Zimmermann concludes, 'answered that he could not decide this for him. The risk had to be taken by him, him alone. If he even spoke of guilt in not making use of a chance, there was certainly as much guilt in light-hearted treatment of the situation. No one could ever emerge without guilt from the situation he was in. But then that guilt was always a guilt borne in suffering.'

Some infer from this one-of-a-kind exchange that Bonhoeffer could not have been a pacifist because, given the opportunity, he backed off. I have myself at times pondered this position but the rest of the evidence in Bonhoeffer's works leads me to conclude this is not the way to read the von Haeften conversation. Rather than evidence for complicity in the assassination conspiracy or even more of a lack of principled pacifism, I see here Bonhoeffer's reticence to say 'Yes, by all means!', as well as his own personal discernment for how he himself was to engage the German situation in the Third Reich. What Bonhoeffer thought right for himself he would not impose on others. So I'm not convinced the von Haeften conversation reveals either Bonhoeffer's supposed realism nor his shift from pacifism, and am convinced, with Mark Thiessen Nation,[13] that he stayed much closer to his christoformic pacifism.

I have worked out my own approach to a peace ethic in four decades of reading Bonhoeffer more than in any other writer. (Other than the New Testament.) But he was the first to turn me to the Sermon on the Mount.

The Sermon and the Peace Ethic

The Sermon on the Mount has been read at times as intensification of law in order to empower confession and repentance, as a dispositional

[13] Nation, Siegrist, and Umbel, *Bonhoeffer the Assassin?*

ethic that turns into momentary insights, as an ethic for the private and not public life or as an ethic for the super-committed but not for all Christians for all times, while others think this is 'discipleship' following the grace of salvation and justification. These approaches do not stand on four legs when the Sermon closes. Respectable, genteel theology is not the way of Jesus. There is no backing off by Jesus at the moment of invitation: he calls people to do what he has said and says those who don't do it will be judged (Matthew 7:13-27).

The seeming impossibility of the fullness of the Sermon is not acknowledged because the rhetoric of Jesus forms into a summons to abandon the ways of Rome and Jerusalem in order to enter into a life shaped by Jesus for those in the kingdom of God. I have in another context written of three dimensions of Jesus' ethic in the Sermon: an ethic from above (where Jesus flat-out tells us what to do as the voice of God), and ethic from beyond (where he expresses an ethic that is beyond our capacity except for moments in this life), and an ethic from below (where he uses wisdom to discern how best to live now). This complicates a peace ethic while it sustains it as the way for those who follow Jesus. I turn now to reflections on the Sermon on the Mount, where I have deepened my sense of a peace ethic.

SEEING THE MARGINALIZED

The Beatitudes of Jesus, though taken over in conversations by virtue ethics, were originally bold expressions of conflict: those whom Jesus approves were not those deemed honorable in the Galilee. While the Matthean version of the Beatitudes (Matthew 5:3-12) does not explicitly recognize the conflictual dimension of these marginalized people, the Lukan version (Luke 6:20-26) makes that conflict obvious. Luke's 'poor' and 'hungry now' and 'weep now' are posed against the 'rich' and the 'full now' and the 'laughing now'. Jesus' blessings are directed not at the high and mighty and powerful, but the lowly and the powerless. This flips the script of who is favored by God. Bonhoeffer's book sent me during a summer at seminary to spend my time studying the term 'blessed', which I examined in the Septuagint and Hebrew Bible. The term refers to divine approval, to an eschatological status that begins now but that will be secured in the final kingdom, to a conditionality of living as that term specifies ('peacemakers'), to a relational ethic in that 'peacemakers' refers to people who mediate peace, and to a reversal – or the conflictual element, that is, to a vision in which those who are presently marginalized by the Roman and Judean and Galilean powers will someday be at the center of God's kingdom. Jesus is the one who decides and declares who is in this kingdom and who is not.

Those who are ignored, suppressed, silenced, and excluded are not just seen by Jesus: he exalts them to center stage. Those who because of exigencies in life do not have the advantages and privileges of others are seen and given a place at the table. Here we find the beginnings of a peace ethic about imprisonment in our society. Here we find the beginnings of a word of grace and hope that can turn prisons, which are populated by folks from the margins, into centers of transformation, reconciliation, and rehabilitation.[14]

PEOPLE OF TOV

Matthew 5 continues with the salt and light, in which we learn that Jesus was calling his followers to be *tov*, the Hebrew word for 'good', and tov people do tov works. Salt is rubbed into 'the land' ('earth' is not the best translation) and light illuminates the 'world', the system of the powers in Rome, Jerusalem and Galilee. Jesus calls his followers not to the ways of the 'land' or the 'world,' but to the ways of a Tov God who calls the people of God to walk in the ways of tov.[15] Being tov runs from the ways of evil (*ra* in Hebrew), and a tov people are intent

---

[14] Aaron Griffith, *God's Law and Order: The Politics of Punishment in Evangelical America* (New Haven, Conn.: Harvard University Press, 2020).

[15] Scot McKnight and Laura Barringer, *A Church Called Tov: Forming a Goodness Culture That Resists Abuses of Power and Promotes Healing* (Carol Stream, Ill.: Tyndale Momentum, 2020).

not on violence and victory over others but on relating to both those in the land and those in the world with grace and goodness. How? By doing tov works, which means public acts of benevolence for the common good. A peace ethic asks what is tov in this situation, which at times transcends what many would perceive to be 'just' or 'right' or even (dare I say it) 'biblical'. It does not ask about status or about who will win, but about what is tov.

FULFILLED IN JESUS

Jesus reads the Bible one way and his opponents another way. They read it as timeless Torah and Jesus reads that same Bible as coming to eschatological fulfillment in himself and in his teachings. The so-called Antitheses of Matthew 5:21-48 clarify a 'righteousness' that 'exceeds that of the scribe and Pharisees' (5:20). In each antithesis we find a hermeneutic: Jesus quotes from the law, he interprets that quotation, he opposes the current tradition of interpretation, he probes the mind of God, and he reveals how his followers are to live. In so doing they follow the eschaton's Messianic lawgiver, now standing on a new Sinai.

The law and the prophets remain God's will, but they are now fulfilled in Jesus, and he fulfills them in himself as Messiah and what he teaches his followers to do. One fulfills the law and the prophets by following Jesus in the whole of his person and life. 'You have heard that it was said' is overmatched by 'But I say to you'. From that mountain on, those who want to do God's will go to Jesus first.

His peace ethic flows out of the courage to let Jesus have the first and final word on how to live. The Way of the Cross, can be inscrutable in moments of despair and discernment when followers of Jesus ask, how do we live in the Way of Jesus in this moment? This question was Bonhoeffer's pervading question for the last decade of his life. A peace ethic then speaks of the primacy of Jesus.

A REVOLUTIONARY HERMENEUTIC

In the six Antitheses that follow, Jesus presents elements of a peace ethic, but to do so he flips the scripts with a revolutionary hermeneutic. The 'plain and simple' reading becomes a surface reading, and Jesus replaces it with a Christocentric reading rooted in his own paradigm of life. I will turn each antithesis into an element valuable for forming a peace ethic, an ethic at the heart of the Way of the Cross. It is not possible here to engage each text in any kind of exegesis.

First, *a peace ethic denounces murder and affirms reconciliation* (Matthew 5:21-26). Nothing could be clearer for a moral life than denouncing murder. To begin there strikes us banal until Jesus turns from the act of murder to the disordered emotion that prompts the eradication of another's life: revenge's anger. Thereby Jesus denounces unjustifiable anger that prompts murder as vengeance. Jesus connects anger and insults because they degrade another person's viability and integrity and identity, and he reforms the prohibition of murder into intentional reconciliation. He touches here what is found in the Lord's Prayer, namely, forgiveness, even if the complexities of forgiveness and reconciliation are left to the side. In the kingdom of God all will be reconciled so Jesus is calling his followers to enter into the peace ethic of forgiveness and reconciliation now. Jesus wants his followers to have a disposition to forgive, he informs them that if they don't forgive, God won't forgive them, that forgiveness has no limit, that forgiveness is effective in social transformation, and that he is himself the paradigm of forgiving others (Luke 11:4; Matthew 6:14-15; 18:21-35; Luke 17:3-4; John 20:23; Luke 23:34). A peace ethic reads the Bible and discerns the right way of life through the lens of creating reconciliation beyond offense, judgment, and punishment.[16]

Second, *a peace ethic, which in this Sermon moved behind act to disordered emotion, recognizes disordered desire behind sexual*

[16] Christopher D. Marshall, *Beyond Retribution: A New Testament Vision for Justice, Crime, and Punishment* (Grand Rapids, Mich.: Wm. B. Eerdmans, 2001); Christopher D. Marshall, *Compassionate Justice: An Interdisciplinary Dialogue with Two Gospel Parables on Law, Crime, and Restorative Justice* (Eugene, Or.: Cascade, 2012).

infidelity and calls followers of Jesus to faithful relations with ordered desires (Matthew 5:27-30). Adultery, considered in the Mediterranean basin as a man's sexual relations with another man's wife – and at times vice versa (Mark 10:12), deepens here to disordered desire: 'everyone who looks at a woman with lust' (Matthew 5:28). He has now caught his entire audience in a kingdom hyperbole that maps onto kingdom realities, where desire will be redeemed and faithfulness practiced. Jesus' remedy is also hyperbolic: tear out the eye that offends and the body parts that desire to be appropriated in the act. A peace ethic calls to a peace-aimed desire.

Third, *a peace ethic urges couples to remain married* (Matthew 5:31-32). Pastor friends of mine no longer preach on this passage when it appears in the lectionary because so many congregants are divorced and remarried. The justifiable divorce clause in our short paragraph, 'except on the ground of unchastity' (or sexual immorality, in a broad sense; 5:32), has been loosened and stretched and expanded to where it is softer than European borders. Jesus counters that very problem in his world. He tightens marriage for kingdom people, without however banning divorce entirely (which was obviously not the problem in his day). The requisite legal release ('certificate of divorce') was all that was required but for Jesus staying together was the summons. Pragmatically, it is better for marriages, for emotional health, and for children for parents to remain married – unless, of course, staying together means sexual violence against one's spouse, emotional violence against one another and family members, and psychological dysfunctions that disturb the emotional development of the children. In which case, a peace ethic releases a woman from a man, and man from a woman, for healing and possible reconciliation or, in some cases, release leading to divorce and a fresh start for all.

Fourth, *a peace ethic leads kingdom people into a world of honesty, truth-telling and transparency* (Matthew 5:33-37). Oaths and vows scaled words from the most truthful to least truthful, the most truthful scale being words buttressed by the name of God. Jesus deconstructs scaling: 'Do not swear at all' (5:34). Let your words be so truthful that one eradicates scaling. Interactions work only because most people tell the truth most of the time but because they don't always tell the truth, we have lawyers. Jesus imagines a world where such judges of truth are no longer needed. Yet, are we called to tell the truth when the Nazis knock on the door to see if we are hiding refugees? When the teacher asks the child in class if a father is an alcoholic? When the pastor is asked by someone if a parishioner is struggling? Jesus here is not offering some reified rule to be followed in all circumstances but is deconstructing a scaling system that legitimates cavalier dismissals of the need to be truth-tellers. A peace ethic calls us to truth-telling.

We come now to direct words about the peace ethic: fifth, *a peace ethic suspends the requirement for balancing the scales of retributive justice* (Matthew 5:38-42). Justice is the fundamental foundation of society. Commensurable punishment, or inflicting a punishment on a perpetrator no more than he or she had inflicted on the victim, is law. In Israelite history punishment was a demand. So vital is this to hear Jesus' own peace ethic, that I want to cite three texts and the italics are mine:

> If any harm follows, *then you shall* give life for life, eye for eye, tooth for tooth, hand for hand, foot for foot, burn for burn, wound for wound, stripe for stripe (Exodus 21:23-25).
> Anyone who maims another *shall suffer* the same injury in return: fracture for fracture, eye for eye, tooth for tooth; *the injury inflicted is the injury to be suffered* (Leviticus 24:19-20).

> *Show no pity*: life for life, eye for eye, tooth for tooth, hand for hand, foot for foot (Deuteronomy 19:21).

I'd like to treat these texts as the world of Jesus did, as God's will for Israel. Moses *demanded punishment in order to establish justice and rectify injustice*. Justice requires retribution. Notice the opening to the words from Deuteronomy: 'Show no pity.' Or, 'No mercy!' Retribution is restricted to a commensurable punishment but the option of non-retribution is absent.

But Jesus says 'But' when he says 'But I say to you, Do not resist an evildoer' (Matthew 5:39). Here Jesus fulfills the law of Moses by turning to a kingdom reality that subverts the legal system's foundation with a new foundation: a peace ethic grounded in grace, forgiveness, mercy, and reconciliation. The term used is non-resistance: 'Do not resist.' In the peace ethic tradition this has been read as 'non-violence' more than simplistic, reified non-resistance. N. T. Wright's *Kingdom New Testament*, in fact, translates 'Don't use violence to resist evil!' Instead of 'Show no mercy', Jesus is saying, 'Show grace.' Grace subverts the power-mongering of Rome.

THE AUDACITY OF PEACE

A peace ethic committed to loving all, including one's enemies, does not respond to militaristic demands as others do. Instead of appealing to rights or demanding justice, Jesus calls kingdom people to decode the system and deconstruct its ways of power by surrendering to the power in a way that removes their teeth and grinding. It is the way of Jesus, after all: he surrendered over and over to the powers, exposed and absorbed their vicious ways on the cross, overcame them into a new life for his followers on Easter Sunday, and empowered them for kingdom living on Pentecost.

Sixth, *a peace ethic converts enemies into neighbors.* For some Israel's scriptures led to a social love for one's own and a social hatred for one's enemies. To put it simpler, to love one's own nation and to despise the nations of others as deplorables and shit-hole countries. Some in the Qumran community saw Rome as the enemy (1QM 1:9-11). The apostle Paul discovered a social hierarchy among Christians (Galatians; Romans 14:1-15:13). Jesus' peace ethic subverts othering gentiles and women and the marginalized and Romans especially and in its place he calls kingdom people to love one's enemies and to pray for one's persecutors. His radical teaching from beyond our time zone does not derive from pragmatics, as if he's saying, 'Hey guys, if we act this way things will go easier for us.' No, he grounds it in the love of God for all humans, and God's love is as wide as the sunshine and as democratic as rain. Which is what he means by 'perfect'.

Ah, now, but what then is 'perfect love'? To love is measured by God's creative love for all. That love is a radical, rugged, and affective commitment to another person to be with them, to be for them, and to participate with them in the fellowship of becoming tov or becoming Christlike.[17]

One who loves as God loves embodies a peace ethic. I did not of course think all

---

[17] Scot McKnight, *Pastor Paul: Nurturing a Culture of Christoformity in the Church*, Theological Explorations for the Church Catholic (Grand Rapids: Brazos, 2019), 41–46. Also, McKnight, *The Jesus Creed*.

these thoughts as a college student when I first was overwhelmed by Bonhoeffer's most famous book, but he gave me direction and courage to root my thinking in the Sermon on the Mount. I have taught it dozens of times, I have read it thousands of times, and I believe it ought to be the foundation for all courses in Christian discipleship. At work in Bonhoeffer's words in that book is the capital idea of participation in Christ, of union with him in his life, of cruciformity and of Christoformity. That, too, formed into an element of my own peace ethic.

3
Gorman and Bonhoeffer

A PEACE ETHIC derives fundamentally from my conviction that the work of God in the life of the Christian, empowered by God's grace through the Spirit and in the context of the community of faith in Jesus, transforms us into Christoformity. Though, as I have said, I first encountered this in Bonhoeffer, Michael Gorman gave me words to think with.[18] One of his most recent crystallizations is this (all italics in Gorman):

> *In the meantime, by the power of the Spirit of Father and Son, the new people, the new humanity bears witness in word and deed to that glorious future by participating now in*

---

[18] Michael J. Gorman, *Cruciformity: Paul's Narrative Spirituality of the Cross* (Grand Rapids: Wm. B. Eerdmans, 2001); Michael J. Gorman, *Participating in Christ: Explorations in Paul's Theology and Spirituality* (Grand Rapids, MI: Wm. B. Eerdmans, 2019).

the life and mission of the triune cruciform God.[19]

Four pages later he says, 'the cross of Christ reveals a missional, justifying, justice-making God and creates a missional, justified, justice-making people.' After 'justice-making' one could add 'peace-making' since Gorman implies peace in the word 'justice'.

Cruciformity as Christoformity

Paul, in his letter to the Romans, connects the Christian's suffering to Christ's suffering and the Christian's future to Christ's own 'future' glory (Romans 8:17). Co-suffering and co-glorification form the heartbeats of Christoformity, which is the eschatological goal of God's work in us. No matter what happens, 'all things work together for good for those who love God' (8:28), and those who love God 'he also predestined to be conformed to

---

[19] Michael J. Gorman, *Becoming the Gospel: Paul, Participation, and Mission* (Grand Rapids, MI: Wm. B. Eerdmans, 2015), 5.

the image of his Son, in order that he might be the firstborn within a large family' (8:29). A slightly more literal translation looks like this:

> Because those whom he knew before
> he also predetermined those [to be]
> co-morphed-to-his-Son's-image
> (so that he is the Firstborn among many siblings).

God's work co-morphs us to be like Christ, what I have learned to call Christoformity, which is a variant of Gorman's penchant, 'cruciformity'.

Christoformity points to a comprehensive redemption in Christ. Our lives are to be like his (bio-formity or mission-formity), our sufferings and deaths are to be like his (cruci-formity), and our resurrection and glorification are to be like his (anastasi-formity). At times we are said to rule with him in the kingdom (archi-formity). Gorman ties Christ to the revelation of who God is so tightly we can also speak of Christoformity as Theo-formity.[20] Christoformity, however, occurs not through valiant efforts or white-knuckling discipline but through the quiet surrender of participation in Christ.

Christoformity and a peace ethic

Christoformity constrains a peace ethic. I cannot comprehend in my heart how a person can kill another or pursue any sort of agenda of death if that person is Christoform or growing into Christoformity. One cannot live for the redemption of the other and put that person down. I cannot, thus, imagine Jesus himself killing a Roman or a Greek or an Alexandria or an Antiochene in a battle. The core themes of my peace ethic are these:[21]

> I cannot kill a non-Christian, for whom Christ has died and to whom I am called to preach the gospel, for the State; that would be rendering to Caesar what is

[20] Gorman, *Inhabiting the Cruciform God: Kenosis, Justification, and Theosis in Paul's Narrative Soteriology*.
[21] From McKnight, *The Sermon on the Mount*, 132.

God's and deconstruct the kingdom mission.

I cannot kill a fellow Christian for the State; that would be rendering to Caesar what is God's. My first allegiance is to the king and to his kingdom people.

I am called to cooperate with the State to the degree it is consistent with the kingdom; I cannot in good conscience cooperate with the State when it is inconsistent with the kingdom; that would be to render to Caesar what is God's.

I cannot ask in the first instance if this is practicable. I am to ask in the first instance what it means to follow Jesus.

This Christoformity shaped in me what I have often called a 'Christoform hermeneutic' that prompts me both to return to a discussion about Bonhoeffer and to a deepening sense of a peace ethic.

A Christform hermeneutic[22]

Debate arises when it is said either that Bonhoeffer was a pacifist or that he remained a pacifist all the way to the end. Bonhoeffer did not affirm pacifism as a 'principle' (*Prinzip*) but I believe he was consistent from his time at Union Theological Seminary in New York (1930-1931) to the end of his life. But the term 'pacifism' does not adequately describe his stance. Instead, he had a Christoform hermeneutic that required specific formation in specific settings. I will explain now how Gorman's cruciformity, my own sense of Christoformity, and Bonhoeffer's hermeneutic led me to a Bonhoeffer-shaped Christoform hermeneutic in a peace ethic.

In 1932, in his lectures in ecumenical work Bonhoeffer clearly articulated a pacifistic stance. In December 1932 before the German

[22] I have written about this in two other locations: 'Jesus, Bonhoeffer, and Christoform Hermeneutics,' *Philosophia Christ* 18 (2016): 221-229; and in a forthcoming Appendix to a book by Mark Thiessen Nation, *Discipleship in a World Full of Nazis*. What follows adapts what I have written there.

Student Christian Movement Bonhoeffer expressed pacifism in classical form:

> The commandment 'You shall not kill,' the word that says, 'Love your enemies,' is given to us simply to be obeyed. For Christians, any military service, except in the ambulance corps, and any preparation for war, is forbidden.[23]

In 1936, in a letter dated 27 January to Elizabeth Zinn, Bonhoeffer confessed he had only recently been converted, which he called his 'grand liberation.' He then said this:

> For me everything now depended on a renewal of the church and of the pastoral station . . . Christian pacifism, which a brief time before ... I had still passionately disputed, suddenly came into focus as

---

[23] A lecture called 'Christ and Peace' and based on student notes taken at that time. See Dietrich Bonhoeffer, *Berlin: 1932-1933*, ed. Carsten Nicolaisen and Ernst-Albert Scharffenorth, DBW 12 (Minneapolis: Fortress, 2009), 260.

something utterly self-evident. And thus it went, step-by-step. I no longer saw or thought about anything else.[24]

To jump ahead, Bonhoeffer was arrested and kept in prison for 18 months because (a) he was accused of deceitfully avoiding military service, and (b) he attempted to keep others from military service.[25] Bonhoeffer operated with one of the most consistently pacifistic christoform hermeneutics in the history of the church. But it was a hermeneutic, not a rule. As a hermeneutic it had to be worked out in specific contexts and I turn now to explore a christoform hermeneutic in the face of dying for others, perhaps the most exacting explication in the history of the church on what

---

[24] Dietrich Bonhoeffer, *Barcelona, Berlin, New York: 1928-1931*, ed. Clifford J. Green, DBW 10 (Minneapolis: Fortress, 2008), 134.

[25] First in the 'Indictment by the Reich War Court' and second in the 'Indictment by the Senior Reich Military Prosecutor,' found in Dietrich Bonhoeffer, *Conspiracy and Imprisonment, 1940-1945*, ed. Mark S. Brocker, trans. Lisa F. Dahill, DBW 16 (Minneapolis: Fortress, 2006), 435–46.

self-denial as participation in Christ means. Here we find utter Christoformity.

Bonhoeffer was against rule-making. Discernment – rather than law-making or undeviating principle-formation – was his method of knowing what to do in a concrete situation. In his *Ethics* he writes,

> To begin quite generally, what is at stake are the times and places that concern us, that we experience, that are realities for us. What is at stake are the times and places that pose concrete questions to us, set us tasks, and lay responsibilities on us ... Against this, however, is the fact that we are placed objectively by our history into a particular context of experience, responsibility, and decision, from which we cannot withdraw without ending up in abstraction.[26]

His 'pacifism' is like the apostle Paul's in Colossians 1:24 when he said, 'Now I rejoice

---

[26] Dietrich Bonhoeffer, *Ethics*, ed. Ilse Tödt and Clifford J. Green, DBW 6 (Minneapolis: Fortress, 2005), 100–101.

in what I am suffering for you, and I fill up in my flesh what is still lacking in regard to Christ's afflictions, for the sake of his body, which is the church.' He goes deeper into his Christoform hermeneutic when he probes into his theory of vicarious representative action [*Stellvertretung*]. That is, his actions of entering into Germany's condition make him guilty but in a christoformic manner that is simultaneously responsible and redemptive for others. This is not imitation of Christ nor is it some kind of moral theory of principles:

> Jesus Christ is the very embodiment of the person who lives responsibly. He is not the individual who seeks to attain his own ethical perfection. Instead, he lives only as the one who in himself has taken on and bears the selves of all human beings. His entire life, action, and suffering is vicarious representative action [*Stellvertretung*].[27]

---

[27] Bonhoeffer, *Ethics*, 231.

On the next page he turns the idea over only slightly to clarify when he says, 'All human responsibility is rooted in the real vicarious representative action of Jesus Christ on behalf of all human beings.'[28] Bonhoeffer's theory of moral *Stellvertretung* then is essentially a Christoform hermeneutic that permits discernment of how to work out Christoformity in a specific situation.

A *Christoform theory of pacifism* is redemptive because it enters into Christ's redemptive vicarious representative act on the cross. Bonhoeffer's abstractions, of which German theology has always been fond, comes clean in this from his *Ethics* when he teaches that (what I am calling) Christoformity is 'an action of vicarious representative responsibility, of love for the real human being, of taking on oneself the guilt that burdens the world.'[29] Christoformity is a hermeneutic for real life decisions by real followers in real situations. Nor is it as simple as 'What would

[28] Bonhoeffer, 232.
[29] Bonhoeffer, *Ethics*, 238.

Jesus do.' Rather we ask, how do I embody the incarnation of God's redemptive love in this moment for this person or persons or situation as one who is in communion with Christ through the Spirit?

4
Craigie

As I was growing into a Christoform peace ethic and hermeneutic, I was challenged by the Old Testament stories of war. I didn't have those words for them in my student days but William Webb and Gordon Oeste's terms do it for me now. Those wars were *Bloody, Brutal, and Barbaric.* Justification of such brutalities had become impossible for me. I wanted an explanation. As a young adult growing up in the Viet Nam era in a church thoroughly unpolitical and yet committed to patriotic ideals like military service, I had no equipment to use for the barbarities when Bonhoeffer's Christoform hermeneutic began to penetrate the marrow of my bones. I pondered in unconscious and unexplored momentary glimpses what to do with those war texts. The old explanation that they were sinners, pagans, and destined for God's judgment lost its credibility. The first book I read on this topic that began to change my mind was by Peter Craigie, *The Problem of War in the Old Testament*.[30] It seemed to settle my conscience but not for long, so over the next forty years I have read a number of books and essays on the topic, the two most recent of which are Greg Boyd's *The Crucifixion of the Warrior God* and Webb and Oeste's *Blood, Brutal, and Barbaric?*,[31] both of which provide light by drawing attention to the hermeneutics of a Christian approach to war in the Bible. In the process of writing an early draft of this book my retired colleague at Northern Seminary, Claude Mariottini, gave me a manuscript of his on this topic and it has become the best solution to the problem of war in the Bible I have yet read.

[30] Peter C. Craigie, *The Problem of War in the Old Testament* (Grand Rapids: Wm. B. Eerdmans, 1978).

[31] Gregory A. Boyd, *The Crucifixion of the Warrior God* (Minneapolis: Fortress Press, 2017); William J. Webb and Gordon K. Oeste, *Bloody, Brutal, and Barbaric? Wrestling with Troubling War Texts* (Downers Grove, Ill.: IVP Academic, 2019).

The problem up close

Many Christians are New-Testament-only Christians. Not by confession but by practices. So removed are they from the Old Testament's realities when they read about them they gasp aloud as if seeing it the first time.

> Then they devoted to destruction by the edge of the sword all in the city, both men and women, young and old, oxen, sheep, and donkeys (Joshua 6:21).

> Now go and attack Amalek, and utterly destroy all that they have; do not spare them, but kill both man and woman, child and infant, ox and sheep, camel and donkey (1 Samuel 15:3).

> Then Israel made a vow to the LORD and said, 'If you will indeed give this people into our hands, then we will utterly destroy their towns.' The LORD listened to the voice of Israel, and handed over the Canaanites; and they utterly destroyed them and their

towns; so the place was called Hormah (Numbers 21:2-3).

At that time we captured all his towns, and in each town we utterly destroyed men, women, and children. We left not a single survivor (Deuteronomy 2:34).

But as for the towns of these peoples that the LORD your God is giving you as an inheritance, you must not let anything that breathes remain alive. You shall annihilate them—the Hittites and the Amorites, the Canaanites and the Perizzites, the Hivites and the Jebusites—just as the LORD your God has commanded (Deuteronomy 20:16-17).

Here are three problem texts about war rape.

Now therefore, kill every male among the little ones, and kill every woman who has known a man by sleeping with him. But all the young girls who have not known a man by sleeping with him, keep alive for yourselves (Numbers 31:17-18).

... and thirty-two thousand persons in all, women who had not known a man by sleeping with him (31:35).

When you go out to war against your enemies, and the LORD your God hands them over to you and you take them captive, suppose you see among the captives a beautiful woman whom you desire and want to marry, and so you bring her home to your house: she shall shave her head, pare her nails, discard her captive's garb, and shall remain in your house a full month, mourning for her father and mother; after that you may go in to her and be her husband, and she shall be your wife. But if you are not satisfied with her, you shall let her go free and not sell her for money. You must not treat her as a slave, since you have dishonored her (21:10-14).

These sorts of texts, taken from Webb and Oeste, became my problems, and though I had (and have) what is often called a 'high' view of

Scripture, there was in my deeper conscience a conviction that these actions were profoundly brutal and barbaric, that my view of Scripture's divine origins was pressing me not to say what seemed obvious, and that any view of Scripture that makes what is immoral and barbaric justifiable has to be wrong itself. Any solution I could find, then, had to see these texts for what they are, not be permitted to swallow them up in some larger justification. In discussing the dark side of the Bible, Greg Boyd admits this:

> I simply cannot find a more polite way of describing, with integrity, portraits of God doing things like causing fetuses to be ripped out of their mothers' womb (Hos 13:16), instigating parents to cannibalize their children (Lev 26:9; Jer 19:9; Lam 2:20; Ezek 5:10; cf. Deut 28:53-57), or commanding his people to merciless massacre entire populations (e.g., Deut 7:2). If portraits of God doing things like this do not qualify as 'horrific,' 'macabre,' or 'revolting,' *what would*?[32]

[32] Boyd, *The Crucifixion of the Warrior God*, 1.290-291.

If you don't agree with that conclusion, then we will have to part company at this point. I find the actions in these texts morally reprehensible. How does one explain such texts?

Explaining the war texts

Webb and Oeste provide a helpful spectrum of five views that I want to summarize briefly before turning to how a Christoform hermeneutic shaped for a peace ethic can 'explain' the texts.[33] One view is that God can do what God damn well pleases. That is, God is sovereign, God is morally free, God is good, God is justice, God punishes sin as the all-holy God, and all that God does is good whether we think so or not. In fact, what we think is good and right and just and loving cannot be used to measure God's goodness, rightness, justice or love. This approach to the war texts implicates God in evil and that is why 'God can do what God damn well pleases' expresses the posture of this view's proponents. It pains me that at one time in my

[33] Webb and Oeste, *Bloody, Brutal, and Barbaric?*, 33–83.

life this viewpoint, which I espoused as the default view, did not pain my morals.

Another view contends the war texts create moral tension. God acts according to his nature, God is not entirely free, but we must admit we don't comprehend reality as God does. What God does is right, and thus these war texts are justified. At the other end of the spectrum are those who somehow repudiate the texts. Knowing Jesus as the fullest revelation of God and who God is leads the discerning reader to see evil in the war texts and to see them as human products and judgments. Hence, the view of God in these texts is inadequate. Even more repudiating than this view, some see these texts as repulsive, the actions abominable, and the God of these texts as a moral monster.

In the middle of these views are other views, like that of Greg Boyd's divine akido/accommodation view as well as Webb and Oeste's incremental, redemptive movement view. I will focus here only on Webb and Oeste since my task is not to present an analytics of viewpoints. In this view there is a combination of the good and the evil, of the ugly and the beautiful. There are then real moral tensions, there is divine accommodation to real world life while there are sign posts pointing us here and there to the fullness of revelation of God in Christ and to the ultimate redemptive ethic of love, peace, and justice. Those moments of breaking through the evil realities of ancient near eastern brutalities prompt hope for fullness of redemption.

A Christoform hermeneutic approach

As I have already stated, the encounter I had already as a college student with Dietrich Bonhoeffer's theology of a Christoform life and then with the explicit challenge by Ronald Sider's defense of a nonviolent approach to resistance on the basis of a cruciform life, put the war texts of the Old Testament into testing ground for the adequacy of Christoformity and the inadequacy of many traditional readings of those war texts. Craigie's attempt to distinguish God's character or moral being from God's participation in history, including its wars, never completely satisfied me while the studies of Boyd and Webb-Oeste, rigorous as they were in admitting the problem and working out a method, have been much more satisfying to me. However, the only satisfying solution for me is to look into the face of God in Christ and from that gaze learn to live in this world in the Way of Christ. When that happens I turn away from the way of war toward a peace ethic fully confident in the power of the Spirit to transcend our inabilities and empower us to live in peace with one another.

I have come to the conclusion that the war texts express human evil at times. My conclusion comes from the Bible's witness to the Way of the Cross. In Christ God has come to humans in all their evil, has entered into that history and reality, has gone all the way to the bottom of that reality in the brutality and hideousness and injustice of Jesus' crucifixion, has unmasked the evil at work in such systems of injustice, has absorbed the injustice in order to redeem its agents (all humans), has redemptively liberated humans from such injustice and evils, has been raised to the world's true Lord, and has sent the Spirit to transform humans into the Way of the Cross, or Christoformity. In Christ God ends the violence of humans by absorbing the violence in his Son for all of us.

Peter Craigie, in his 1978 book *The Problem of War in the Old Testament,* offered conclusions similar to my argument here, but he is worthy of being quoted in full. Out of his discussion of the realistic portraits of war in the Old Testament and the inability of those social institutions to lead into the kingdom of God, he concluded:

> But the establishment of the Kingdom of God in the person of Jesus reveals to us a new understanding of violence; the tables are turned. Whereas the old kingdom was established by the *use* of violence, the new Kingdom was established in the *receipt* of violence. God the Warrior becomes the Crucified God, the one who receives in himself the full force of human violence.

Here he sounds like what will be seen in my colleague Claude Mariottini. What pained Craigie is what too many Christians have forgotten or failed to understand or, sadly, flat-out rejected:

> Over and over again, Christians have forgotten that God the Warrior became the Crucified God.[34]

That shift makes use of what I call a 'Christoform hermeneutic'. Everything changes. In the meantime, we live in a world racked with evil and injustice and barbaric brutalities. In that meantime, we look forward in hope to the New Jerusalem while we strive now for the peace ethic of that New Jerusalem in our world today. Those who have seen God in the face of Jesus can do no other, even if they must stand against the ways of the empire in this world.

---

[34] Craigie, *The Problem of War in the Old Testament*, 99–100.

5
Collins

For some critics of the kind of peace ethic so far explained, the Book of Revelation's portrait of the so-called violence of Jesus both defeats the various explanations and establishes an entirely different – a legitimate Christian use of a just violence – explanation of the passages so far discussed. For them, the best path to peace is to ready your country for war.

Many make this claim. Tremper Longman, a prolific Old Testament scholar, said, 'Jesus in the New Testament is no less violent than the revelation of God in the Old Testament' and he contended that the Book of Revelation appears to be more violent than wars of the Old Testament.[35] Of course, if violence is bad then

---

[35] Tremper Longman III, 'A Response to C.S. Cowles,' in *Show Them No Mercy: Four Views on God and the Canaanite Genocide*, ed. Stanley N. Gundry (Grand Rapids, Mich.: Zondervan, 2003), 58.

Longman's claim impugns both the Old and the New Testaments. The view is as rooted in a theory of Scripture as anything else: since the Old Testament is inspired, etc., then what it says of God is true and that means a violent interpretation of Revelation is compatible with the violent God of the Old Testament. Furthermore, this hermeneutic is too flat: as we have shown, Jesus did not accept the scriptures at face value but instead offered a hermeneutic that begins with who he is and what he says, and the apostles developed that hermeneutic into what I have called a Christoform hermeneutic.

The question, however, remains: Is the Jesus of Revelation violent and, if so, does that violence contradict the Christoform hermeneutic? I will propose some considerations after a brief sketch of the so-called violence of Revelation. We need not go outside Revelation 19:11-21. Here the white horse rider is Jesus, and he 'makes war'. His cloak is 'dipped in blood' and he is accompanied by heaven's armies. A 'sharp sword' flows from his mouth 'to strike down the nations', over which he reigns 'with a rod of iron.' Noticeably, drawing on the language of the prophets, 'he will tread the wine press of the fury of the wrath of God the Almighty'. The next scene is gore, the stuff of Marvel movies and Homer's famous epics: the birds gather to pick at the flesh of the defeated. Then a battle with the 'beast and the kings of the earth and their armies' but here the beast and the false prophet are captured and tossed 'alive into the lake of fire'. Everyone else was killed and the birds gorge themselves on the corpses.

Thinking about Revelation

Apocalyptic literature famously deals with a singular problem: the claim of God's sovereignty and the reality of injustice against the people God who make that claim.[36] That the problem is God's sovereignty is as true of Revelation as it is true of any Jewish apocalypse, the major difference being that this one is about the seven churches of western Asia Minor.

---

[36] In what follows, I use John J. Collins, *Apocalypse, Prophecy and Pseudepigraphy: On Jewish Apocalyptic Literature* (Grand Rapids, Mich.: Wm. B. Eerdmans, 2015), 310–14.

The violence of Revelation fits into typical expressions of cosmic and earthly battles between good and evil. God always wins, the evil forces of the cosmos always lose. Apocalyptic literature routinely gets accurately tagged with language like 'symbolic' and 'imagery' and 'metaphor'. Which ought at least to make readers wonder if the language is not fiction. In fact, a case can be made that apocalyptic imagery of battles won by God and battles lost by the forces against God and God's people trades in some fantasy and fiction.

The obscure small house churches of western Asia Minor certainly can't genuinely entertain the option that they will defeat mighty Rome. Revelation indulges their hope by fashioning fantasies of victory in order to spur them on to faith, hope, and active witness. Yes, of course, it is not pure fiction like *Lord of the Rings*. No, it is the kind of fiction that is real-er than the real because it carries the message that someday Babylon will go down and New Jerusalem will come. In other words, the arc of divine providence's history bends toward justice, but it is a justice accomplished by God not by military victory.

Such fantasies of violent defeat trade in stock images of the ancient world in which moral battles are waged by earthly figures in well-known locations with gruesome endings symbolizing the good guys conquering evil. As such, John Collins helps us by speaking of these fantasies as therapeutical and cathartic.[37] Nothing soothes the oppressed more than defeating injustice. While we may sit in judgment on this language today we need at least to pause to observe that children love the victories of *The Chronicles of Narnia*, *The Lord of the Rings*, and *Harry Potter* – and dare I add adults too! Top that with the audiences of the Marvel movies and one has the same audiences that loved *The Iliad* and *The Odyssey* and *The Aeneid* and, yes, the Book of Revelation. Elisabeth Schüssler Fiorenza long ago observed that this appeals to the oppressed and offends only those who are

---

[37] Collins, 333–36.

privileged enough not to be oppressed.[38]

What is more is that this violence is not human but divine. As John Collins expresses it, 'By enabling people to let off steam by fantasizing divine vengeance, it relieves the pressure toward action in the present and enables people to accommodate themselves to the status quo for the present.'[39] Which brings us to the divine victory of the Lamb, the Logos of God. What is noticeable and can't be missed is that the white horse rider's weapon is a sword the comes from the mouth. This is not a sword in the fist of a military warrior but the Logos of slaying evil with the Logos. The blood-drenched robe, taken by many as indicative of a military slaughter, has been read by many as the Lamb's blood, the Lamb slaughtered for the redemption of every tribe and nation and tongue. Here we have the Way of the Word, not the Way of the Sword.

Add now this: many are addicted to a literal

[38] Elisabeth Schüssler Fiorenza, *Revelation: Vision of a Just World*, Proclamation Commentaries (Minneapolis: Fortress, 1992).

[39] Collins, *Apocalypse, Prophecy & Pseudepigraphy*, 321.

reading of many of these images even when they reject the commonly-derided literal readings of American classical dispensationalism. Once one rejects the literalistic reading, the reader is obliged to carry through a consistent symbolic reading, and once the Book of Revelation is appreciated for its fantastical and metaphorical readings the 'violence of Jesus' becomes nonviolence. Imagery of violence? To be sure. But why? Because these sorts of battle are how apocalyptic rolls. It is an open question whether or not such violent images spur people onto violence. Without denying the possibility and realities, the evidence is not as much in favor of precipitating violence as some claim.[40] Once one rejects the literal reading and sees Revelation's images of Jesus, the Warrior-Lamb-and-Logos, as fictional presentations

---

[40] Collins, 336–42. Which is not to say it is never used to legitimate violence. See throughout Philip Gorski, *American Covenant: A History of Civil Religion from the Puritans to the Present* (Princeton: Princeton University Press, 2019); Andrew L. Whitehead and Samuel L. Perry, *Taking America Back for God: Christian Nationalism in the United States* (New York: Oxford University Press, 2020).

of a future reality when God's justice will be established, the so-called violence of Jesus diminishes to the point of evaporation.

A final observation: many readings of Revelation miss its progression. For instance, the lake of fire. Many get lost here in the vacuum of discussing belief in and the nature of hell, and whether Revelation teaches eternal conscious punishment or annihilation (conditional immortality). The Book of Revelation has a narrative flow: the lake of fire is where evil is erased *so the New Jerusalem can come.* What is any more true than this: *for justice to be fully formed injustice must be eliminated*? The rhetorical functions of the fantasies and imageries of Revelation are to encourage the oppressed people of God in western Asia Minor and to assure them that someday the arc of God's apocalyptic history will establish justice and Babylon's tyrannical evils will be extinguished.

In the meantime

The all-too-common speculative readings of Revelation are obsessed with identification

THE AUDACITY OF PEACE

(Who is the antichrist? Which city today is the future Babylon?) and expectation (Is the European Union not a fulfillment of the endtime alliance against the people of God?). What follows for the Christians who read Revelation like this? Relief that they are to be raptured or fear that they will be left behind.[41] But this completely fails the discipleship teachings of Revelation.

Interleaving the central chapters of the book (4-19) are songs, which can be read as an early version of America's slave who sang Spirituals. The Songs of Revelation instruct believers how to think and worship and sing while living in Babylon. They are to learn to sing that God is on the throne and join the chorus that says,

> The kingdom of the world has become the
> kingdom of our Lord
> and of his Messiah,
> and he will reign forever and ever
> (Revelation 11:15).

[41] Amy Johnson Frykholm, *Rapture Culture: Left Behind in Evangelical America* (New York: Oxford University Press, 2004).

This creates for them an alternative social imaginary. This leads their worship to be a witness of both works and word in which they declare in a lived theology that Caesar is not their lord. Jesus is!

The discipleship theme at the heart of Revelation then is dissidence and subversion of the ways of Rome – led by the Dragon, implemented by the Beasts from the land and the sea, and embodied in Babylon. Babylon's marks are: (1) imperialism, (2) idolatry, (3) opulence, (4) status, (5) arrogance, (6) power, (7) military might, (9) murder, and (10) economic exploitation. In the middle of that the seven churches are summoned by the lordly colossus called Jesus to witness in their works and in their words to this alternative reality that they learn to see by being ushered into God's Throne Room.

They do this first in their small house church gatherings: they embody the Way of the Lamb and they resist as dissident disciples the way of the Dragon. Their habits emerge over time into a living reality, the agency of goodness in the Way of the Lamb. So emergent is this living reality of goodness that goodness itself becomes an agent constraining the believers to act in all spheres of life as those who have learned an alternative reality. That is, when they enter the agora they behave not as Romans but as Christoform humans. They worship God, they are not driven by power and opulence and status and arrogance, they resist military victories, and they choose the ways of economic generosity and equity.

That is the peace ethic of Revelation. It is the Way of the Lamb and the challenge is to follow the Lamb while living in Babylon.

We've come to the end. I have wended my way into a peace ethic by learning from thinkers like Ronald Sider, Dietrich Bonhoeffer, Michael Gorman, and Peter Craigie. Each led me to a deeper perception the simple words of Jesus to take up the cross.

The Way of the Cross is not the Way of the Sword.